Before and After

Karla Esteban-Conopio

BookLeaf
Publishing

Presentation by *BookLeaf Publishing*

Web: www.bookleafpub.com

E-mail: info@bookleafpub.com

ISBN: 978-93-95755-58-0

First edition 2022

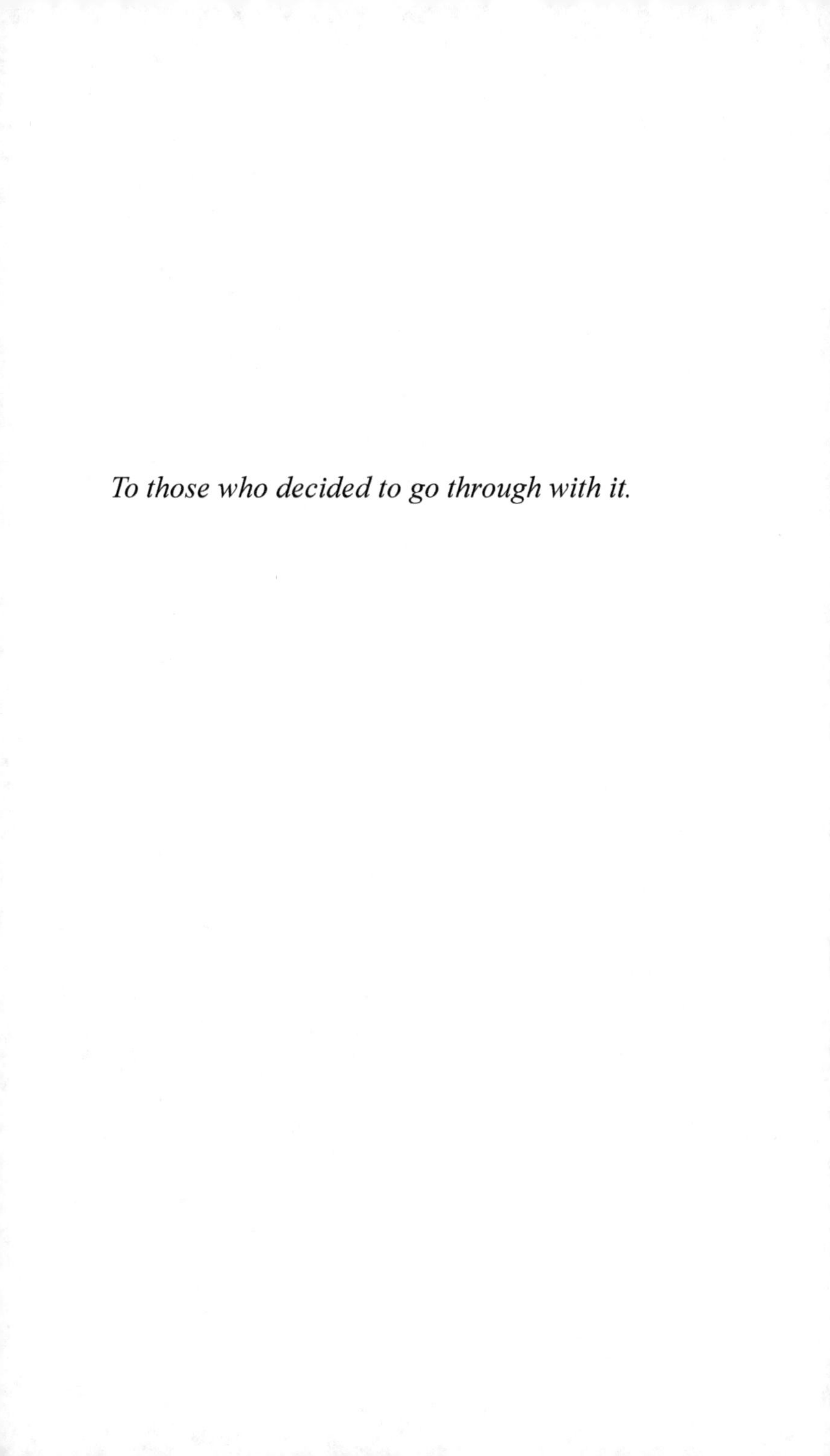

To those who decided to go through with it.

ACKNOWLEDGEMENT

I wish to acknowledge the great people that I now call friends at Primary Health Care Corporation. The place has given me a lot of inspiration and creativity, not all good, but pertinent to my musings. I would also like to thank my high school UPHD, where my love for writing started. I would love to thank my sisters, KC and KT, who I miss dearly; my parents who made sure I honed my talents. I would also like to thank my spouse, my best friend, who always brings me my coffee when I want it, and who is currently playing video games and waiting for me to join in.

Sleepless

Just like how the sunlight catches the motes that at one moment were not there

A distant memory, forgotten, finally creeping its way up.

Knocks at 1 AM and ask for you to remember.

You lose sleep.

…

And you lose sleep.

You toss and turn, trying to forget. But the more you try, the harder it is to forget.

You wish it wasn't a memory, or wish you had a faulty one.

Cause it can't seem to have happened the way you're remembering it at 1 am.

And still, you're awake, forced to remember. You shut your eyes…

God how awful it must have been

Cause the black canvas your shut eyes have
created had been colored with your memory

Then it's daylight.

You see the sunbeam break through the window

And the motes danced in their light

Tempus Fugit

Time does not heal.
Time is a measurement.
Time measures how long you waited for
someone who did not come.
Time measures how long you slept in.
Or it measures how long it took for you to
finally doze off.
Or how long you've been crying.
Time does not heal.
Time is not reliable when you need healing.
Time can only give itself.
So, accept it. Cry until your eyes hurt,
Or until you get tired. But do not take forever.
Because time does not wait.

Mull things over in a hot bath,
Until your palms get wrinkly.
Drown yourself in alcohol.
Cry on the floor, on your bed.
But do not take forever.
Because one day, you will be the one
Who will push yourself off the floor,
Who will give up the bottles,
Who will go out and face friends,

Who will dry yourself from the one-hour baths.

It is you who heals yourself.
It is you who gets up.
It is you who forces yourself out of exhaustion.
It is you who gets tired of hurting.
Because in the end,
When someone asks you,
"How did you do it?"
You do not say "Time healed me."
Say "I just did."

Retrospect

5

A bit of yesterday fell today

Bared its teeth,

Showed promises it has yet to keep.

A bit of yesterday breathed down my spine.

Whispered words,

I used to believe all the time.

A bit of yesterday knocked on my door,

Clawed its way in,

When I refused to hear its lore.

A bit of yesterday filled my thoughts

"Here have more"

Decided to live there, ate up all my core.

Yesterday, little by little,

Forgotten and neglected.

Yesterday is but a memory, a torrential
conscious regret.

We Are

We are the hollows of our throats.
As deep as the oceans, but as far as the shores.
The words that seem to roll off your tongue
Seem to slide into mine,
As though I was yours
As though you were mine
Then I was yours
Then you were mine
Until we no longer know which end begins and
follows.

We are the stars in the tapestry above
Individually burning but we are constellations.
Far apart yet seem to reach out.
Ablaze and burning, raging, raging, raging.

We are the days and the minutes
The table-time discussions
The wonder and the wander
The names that we breathe down our neck.
How much more love is there to give?

A break and a pause, and semantic satiation.
A beat, a step, and repeat over again.
As days come shorter, and weeks much faster

We anticipate, restless and longing.
We are the spaces that we fill in between.
We are the words that never lacked meaning.

Days come nearer, my dear, I will be the wave
and you the shore.

Figment

I have ideations.
>Fantasies of long necklaces,
>Which adorns me while I chill.
>Of bracelets as thick as curdled blood
>And bright as MAC's Ruby Woo.

Ideations:
>Of flying and landing on the asphalt.
>Bones crackle from the free fall.
>Splayed across the floor.

Fantasies:
>Of ephemeral dreams
>And ethereal realities
>Of not waking up
>Slowly mixing tonics and drugs.

I have ideations.
>They whisper to me, or
>Vividly shows a picture of me
>Cold-hearted, pale, and lackluster.

I close my eyes.
>Hide under the sheets,
>And make fists from my hands.

Waiting…

Am I still going to wake up tomorrow?

Toska

A morning call somewhere far below,
Hollow and a frightening mess.
A cloud appears above your head,
And then your walls undress.

There's a pompous rat
Wriggling to be free.
Try to scurry past defenses,
But defenses are futile, they are weak.

It's a steady hymn lilting through,
A passion it has become.
While others associate it with the color blue,
You have come undone.

Mondays, afternoons, in the dead of the night,
It chooses no time to follow you.
Then auspiciously it takes flight,
With a promise to return to you.

What is it? 'tis a mystery.
A mystery or a misery,
A riddle or something morbidly messy,
Never laugh, it is never funny.

A Different Stanza

Allow me to break your heart
Set things straight, but not quite now.
Be one with the heavens above,
Something pure right from the start.

Be gentle like the breeze,
A song that's now heard.
See me as the most complex,
See me as plain as this.

Aren't we an odd set?
Lost to a life I thought sufficed.
Agreeing to all sorts of nonsense,
Aren't you glad of the butterfly effect?

Allow me to give you a piece of me,
Bit by bit, a whole for free.
Piece them together,
Surprise! You have me.

Here's to endless discussions
And more things in common.
Here's to filling spaces and gaps,
Midway points and more destinations.

Set things straight now should start,
We keep things light and easy.
I kid of breaking your heart,
Though it breaks me when we part.

To you I say, never doubt nor worry
But perfect words seem to leave me.
A smile I give to fill the silence....
I will always stay.

Sun Rays are Pretty

15

Like dust.
It was only dust. What we have.
Or what we had.
It was never really there unless you shed some
light into it.
Like when the sun rays make way for the dust.
Lighting them, fleeting.
Forever replaced.
And like dust, it was meaningless.

California Maki

What my eyes could not see,
I trust yours would.
Just help me move
So, this will help you move.

We are young and free.
There is so much time to mingle.
I am not the only one
Your heart would choose.

Let this be a lesson learned.
Change for the right reasons.
Change to be a better person.
Change for the next big thing.

Change for the person you're
Going to fall in love with next.
We had it and we lost it.
Let us learn from it and cherish it.

Let us set each other free.
If it is true that we are for each other,
Then let us wait and give it time.
Let us be patient.

I hope you have learned your lesson
As i have learned mine.
I have nothing more to remind me of you.
Just what it felt to be with you.
Soon, I will forget.
Thanks to my erratic memory.

Motes

I hope someday the stars fade out
As soon as my head touches the pillow,
And worries and wonders soon slurry
As I wait for the morrow.

May that itch that cannot be scratched
Or the confusion I get in the morning sun
And the questions I keep asking
Clear out with a cup of joe.

May the pills I took and the ones I didnt
Meant something for my disposition.
I could care less now but to be honest,
I know that I am wrong.

Time doesn't heal and it doesn't wait
Time makes fun of me in a way.
It's a wonder how time is all I got
And not what I have at the same time.

May I someday rest,
Though despondent at life,
Be at peace knowing,
With difficulty, I have done my best.

I hope to continue reminding myself
That I am but a speck dancing under the rays
And all those that bring joy and sorrow
Are mirages in the haze.

On the Day I Died

The day after I died,
I walked the path where the flowers bloomed
Beneath my feet.

I felt the blades of the grass,
the dew the formed, and the icy air,
and the birds that flew to greet.

The day I died,
I saw the waves crash down the beach,
Recede as soon as it came.

The salty air, I immediately recognized.
The sand on my soles, the shells I collected
The droplets I felt as it rained.

The day I died,
I took the trail up the highest mountain.
And saw the clouds that were within reach.

As I see the sunset across the horizon
It felt like the first time I saw them.
Then I realized these were things I have missed.

The day I died,

I wish I could take the time away from myself.
And have done it at the eleventh hour

Now it's late,
I have seen what I have missed and what could
have been
But my life had made it sour.

The day I died,
The rivers continued to flow
Did not seem to notice my leave

The world continues to go on so I've seen,
And no one seems to grieve.

Triad

Your absence feels like a cold touch
I reach for your space
But that did not do much
Only memories linger, they run at a slow pace.
An airless dust swivels in place.

I wish the last words were not last
I wish it was a song waiting for its completion
But things, you, left too fast
Now my memory feuds with what I wished for
and what has passed.

The faulty memory box I opened
I saw your laughter, but just the happy ones.
I should have listened to the in-betweens, to
fleeting moments
but mostly unnoticed.

I wish I'm remembering differently now
But maybe I'm choosing to do so
All I could ask now is how
And all answers only point to you,
Joy, Sorrow, Regret

Tryst

Sweat drips a lovely dew
Across the brow and onto you
What happens next
Let me in
I'm too invested
Lips are sealed

A touch so warm
This can go all night
A furious thump
A nightly howl
But say again,
My name out loud.

I succumb to what happens next
I came upon your acid wreck
This is but a moment, a second.
I wish it would end on a higher scale
So, I can capture your embrace
And your hungry gaze turned to haze.

Grow onto me
And latch on to my arch
Be satisfied with me on top
I'll reach the heavens

Just for you
But let me in
I'll come through.

Yonder

There's light I could never reach
Far atop I gaze upon
But stand tall as I might
It grows farther on

I've been told various advice
But meaningless and devout
Have not worked on me
The light grows farther as you can see

I've been told to just extend
my arms to reach
But my arms can only do so much
The light grows farther from me.

The only comfort I get
Is seeing the light
Far from me but grows stronger still
I wish it would come closer to me

I've forgotten
the darkness around me
Too focused on the light
As it steps away from me

I wish to seek other places
I wish there were more to see
Maybe this is not the only light
That my faint eyes can see.

Vow

A light-hearted talk,
An easy afternoon
A cup of black,
To an already dark heart.

With you, a smile,
Could easily start
A whole new chapter,
And ease the heart

Who knew a life
Like this exists
Who knew that there
Is a lot I missed.

Every battle that I've been
And scars I have gained
Were replaced with laughter
Even as it rains.

You took down my walls
Only to bring them back up again
But with you inside
And there remained.

You have added windows
To let the sunshine in.
Added the door,
To let people come, or out if they sin.

The roof you've built
To protect us from the past.
A huge kitchen,
For the future's dish cast.

You are here,
All present and with me.
I see you, every crack, every bone.
Cause you are what I call home.

7/11

I sold my soul,
Under fluorescent lights
Just one look
Cursed now are my nights

I picked a fight
With a heart not the same
I wish to take it back
And keep it tame

I smile and hide
But bright are the lights
Every nook will be seen
My truths are shown quite so bright.

Take it back
I wish I could
My heart, my soul, my previous life
Just to be rid of this wound.

Quiet and lonely
This will be
But I should pay
For the sin that is me.

I see that I cannot repay
Any costs the devil relay.
But my soul then I freely give
So that I could truly live.

Daybreak

I wish I still love you
When tomorrow comes.
When all the worries
Ended at midnight.

When anger resets
At the break of dawn.
When ideals change
At the change of the hour.

I wish I still you you
When I have forgotten,
What problems we have
And promises are broken.

When kisses suffice
A lonely heart
When words comfort
And opens a new start.

I wish I still love you,
When I open my eyes
After tears have fallen
And forgotten lies.

After hearing you say
Apologies and promises
After being together
Or a long embrace.

I wish I still love you
But I cannot lie
The warmth has left me
And felt it has died.

There are no promises
I want to hear.
No embrace I could stand,
Or tomorrows to hold dear.

If the day next does arrive,
I'll see myself out.
I will take the baggage
As that is tantamount.

I wish I could love you,
That has long gone.
Slowly and surely
This was eventually done.

Paint

I stare at my walls
As my mind wanders into things,
As tears fall,
As I muffle my whimpers.

The paint on my wall is uneven
And I see the patterns
Unravel before my eyes
Like secrets meant for no one.

A girl laughs at me as I wallow in pain.
A tiger ready to pounce.
A mermaid I created long ago,
Gone forever but not in thoughts.

They leave as soon as they had come.
A different character transforms.
A different pattern evolves,
Changes from one shape to another.

I can change too as everyone does.
I built walls around me
And I will unravel before my very eyes.
Like those patterns on my wall.

www.ingramcontent.com/pod-product-compliance
Lightning Source LLC
LaVergne TN
LVHW010022200726
843495LV00015B/1880